TOOLS for OBSERVING

By Illa Podendorf

Illustrations by Donald Charles

 CHILDRENS PRESS, CHICAGO

Illa Podendorf, former Chairman of the Science Department of the Laboratory Schools, University of Chicago, has prepared this series of books with emphasis on the processes of science. The content is selected from the main branches of science —biology, physics, and chemistry—but the thrust is on the process skills which are essential in scientific work. Some of the processes emphasized are observing, classifying, communicating, measuring, inferring, and predicting. The treatment is intellectually stimulating which makes it occupy an active part in a child's thinking. This is important in all general education of children.

This book points up the importance of tools that are commonly used to extend the powers of observation by sight and touch. The microscope, telescope, scale, balance, thermometer, and ruler are a few that are presented.

Library of Congress Catalog Card Number: 73-160599

1 2 3 4 5 6 7 8 9 10 11 12 13 14 15 16 17 18 19 20 21 22 23 24 25 R 75 74 73 72 71

CONTENTS

TOOLS FOR OBSERVING LITTLE THINGS

Joe found a butterfly
that could not fly.

He picked it up.

He was surprised to see
that the wings left dust
on his fingers.

He looked closely at the
dust. A little of it was
black. A lot of it was
orange.

He used a hand lens
to look at the dust. It
looked bigger. Each tiny
piece was longer than it
was wide.

Joe decided it was not
dust.

Joe wanted to see the
dust more clearly.

His brother showed him
how to put two hand lenses
together.

Now the tiny bits looked
bigger. Joe could see
that all the bits were
shaped alike. They were
almost rectangular. But
each had points on it.

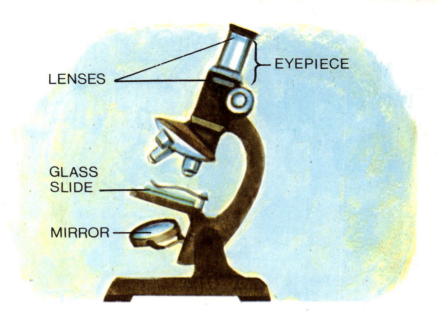

LENSES

EYEPIECE

GLASS
SLIDE

MIRROR

Joe and his brother had a
good idea. They would use
a microscope to look at the
dust.

A microscope has more than
one lens. They are held firmly
in place. If they are strong
lenses, the dust can be seen
clearly.

They put a little of the
dust on a glass slide. Then
they put the slide under the
lens of the microscope.

The boys moved the mirror to focus the light in the microscope. Then they moved the lenses up and down until they could see the dust clearly.

"Dust is not a good name for those tiny bits," said Joe.

"Tiny bits is not a good name either," said his brother. "I think scales is a better name."

Joe looked at the butterfly wing through the microscope.

He could see where some scales had been lost.

Joe looked through a
microscope at a thread.

He looked at a feather.

He looked at the edge
of a piece of grass.

Without a microscope, Joe never would have seen scales from a butterfly's wing.

With the help of a microscope, Joe really saw many things for the first time.

Scientists know about many things, because they have microscopes.

They know about cells in our bodies.

They know about harmful germs. They can see them with the help of a microscope.

Some scientists study plants under a microscope.

Joe put a drop of water
from a ditch on a glass slide.

He covered it with a small
glass slide.

He saw many interesting
things swimming around. They
were very small animals.

He saw green bodies, too.
They were tiny plants.

TOOLS FOR OBSERVING FAR-AWAY THINGS

Telescopes have lenses
in them, too. They do not
make things look bigger than
they are. They make them
look closer than they are.

You have seen the moon
when it looked like this.

Through a telescope, it
may look like this.

Mars looks like a big star when you
see it in the sky.   It is
really a planet.

A telescope seems to bring it closer.

MARS

Mars looks like this through
a big telescope. Can you see
the snowcaps?

SATURN

Joe visited a place called a planetarium. He saw the moon and Mars and other planets as they would look through a telescope. He saw the rings around Saturn.

PLANETARIUM

TOOLS FOR FINDING WEIGHTS

Joe held a young guinea pig in one hand. He held its mother in the other hand. He thought the young guinea pig felt almost as heavy as its mother. The young guinea pig was growing fast.

How could he know when it was as heavy as its mother.

He decided to use a scale.

The scale showed that the mother guinea pig weighed about a pound and a half. This was the pull of gravity on it.

The baby guinea pig weighed
a little less than a pound. This
was the pull of gravity on it.

Joe made a scale.
He hung up a spring
securely. He fastened
a strip of paper behind
it.

Then he hung a small
bag on the end of the
spring.

He made a mark on the
paper at the end of the
spring.

Each time he put a
marble in the bag, the
spring stretched.

Each time the spring
stretched, Joe made a
mark on the paper.

These marks were his
units of weight.

Then Joe took
the marbles out
of the bag.

He put a ball
in it.

He could say
that the ball
weighed eight
marbles.

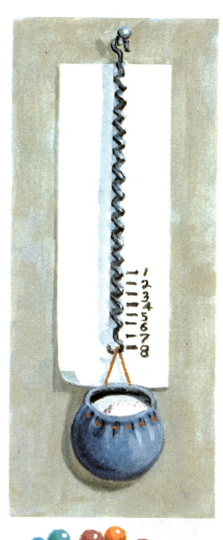

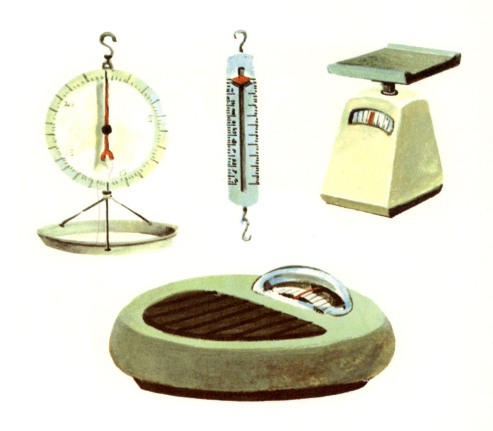

All scales tell how hard the earth's gravity is pulling on something. There are many kinds of scales. They are all important tools for observing weight.

Did you ever weigh yourself? Could you find your weight without a scale?

This astronaut weighs about 180 pounds on the earth. Would he weigh that much on the moon?

You are sure to say that he would not.

The moon's gravity is only one sixth as great as that of the earth. Can you find out how many pounds this astronaut would weigh on the moon?

TOOLS FOR FINDING MASS

You have been finding
the weight of things by
measuring the pull of
gravity with a scale.

The weight of something
may change because of
where it is.
On the moon,
an astronaut weighs less
than he does on the earth.

But his mass does not
change. There is just as
much of him on the moon
as there is of him on
the earth.

Joe had a glove in one hand,
and a ball in the other. He thought
they felt as though one would balance
the other.

This is a balance. It is a valuable
tool for finding the mass of something.
Joe used it to see whether the ball and
the glove balanced.

Joe made a balance. You can see from the picture how he did it.

He hung washers on each end of the balance. See how many small washers balance the one big washer.

You can make a balance, too.

    You can find the mass of
something when you balance it
with standard units.

    You can use pieces of metal
that are equal to certain numbers
of grams. They are called gram
masses. Grams are used in the
metric system. They are standard
units.

    It would take about 28 grams
to balance an ounce of candy.

How many masses balance this
mother hamster? Three?

Do the three masses equal 75 grams?

Joe found that a young hamster balanced
45 grams.

How many grams of apple are on
this balance?

How many gráms of popcorn are
on this balance?

A balance is a tool for observing.
It helps us find the masses of things.

TOOLS FOR OBSERVING TEMPERATURES

It is easy to see that the icicles
in the sunshine are melting.

It is warmer in the sunshine
than it is in the shade.

Joe can tell by the feel of it that his soup is hot.

He can tell that his milk is cold.

But he cannot tell how hot and how cold they are without a tool.

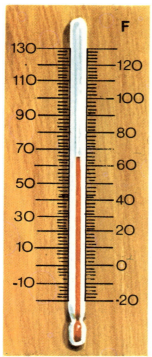

This thermometer is marked with the Fahrenheit scale.

This thermometer is marked with the Celsius scale.

Both are tools for telling temperature.
The unit of measure is the degree.
A degree is larger on the Celsius scale
than it is on the Fahrenheit scale.

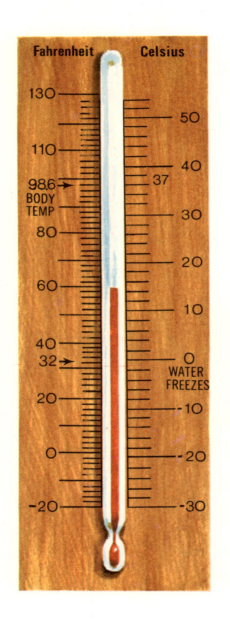

Fahrenheit

130

110

98.6 →
BODY
TEMP

80

60

40

32 →

20

0

-20

Celsius

50

40

37

30

20

10

0
WATER
FREEZES

-10

-20

-30

What is the freezing temperature on each of these thermometers?

What is the boiling point on each of them?

What is normal body temperature on each of them?

Scientists use the Celsius scale.

Weather reports are usually given in Fahrenheit scale. Sometimes they are given in both scales.

One of these thermometers makes a
graph of the temperature it takes.
Can you tell which one it is?

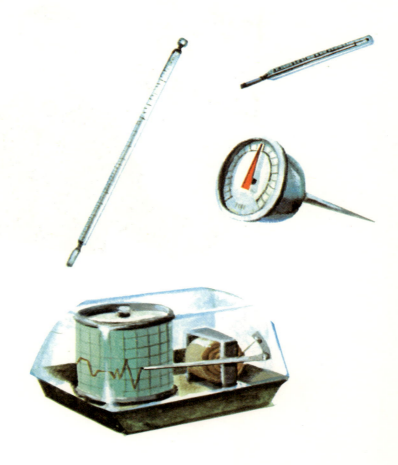

TOOLS FOR TELLING TIME

You know that it is morning when the sun comes up. But if you want to know when it is time to go to school, you need a watch or a clock to tell you.

OIL LAMP

STRIPED CANDLE

HOUR GLASS

WATER CLOCK

BURNING KNOTTED ROPE

People used many tools for telling time before there were watches and clocks.

A sundial shows the time of day
by the shadow it makes.

Joe made a simple sundial
with a stick and some stones.
Can you tell the time his
sundial is showing?

TOOLS FOR OBSERVING SHAPES AND SIZES

It is easy to see that Joe's little brother is not as tall as Joe is.

Joe will need to use a tool to see exactly how tall his little brother is.

Joe used a yardstick to measure his brother. His brother was a little more than three feet tall. You could also say that he was a little more than a yard tall.

Then Joe used a metric ruler. His brother was exactly one meter tall.

Scientists always use the metric system for measuring. Someday we will be using it all the time.

It is more easily used because the units are smaller. It is also easy to use because the units are in tens.

Decimeter

Ten centimeters equal one decimeter. Ten decimeters equal one meter.

Joe could see that one lollipop
stick was longer than the other.
He measured them.
One was 8 centimeters long.
One was 10 centimeters, or
1 decimeter long.

Joe wanted to see if some circular shapes were really circular. He used his tool called a compass.

He could see that one of the shapes was not a good circular shape. Do you know which one it was?

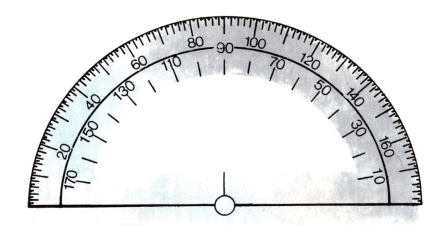

This is a protractor. Joe uses
it to measure angles.

Could he tell which of these
angles is larger without a
protractor?

This tool is called a level.
It has a bubble in a little tube
of water.

Builders use this tool. It helps
them see whether a board is level.

If the board is higher at one end,
the bubble moves that way.

Joe made a level. He used a
tall glass bottle filled to the
top with water.

You can make one, too. You may
have to try several times to get
a small bubble.

SOME THINGS TO DO

Make a list of other tools for observing.

Did you think of a rear-view mirror? A periscope? A prism? Eye-glasses?

Look at salt through a hand lens. Put two lenses together and look at the salt again. Look at other little things.

Make a scale like the one on page 20.

Make a balance like the one on page 27. How many small washers equal a large washer? Balance other things.

Put a few drops of pond water on a slide. Look at it under a microscope. What can you see that you could not see before?

Get several glasses of water. Write down what you think the temperature is of each one. Use a thermometer and find out how nearly right you were.

Make a leveling tool like the one Joe made on page 47.

Write down your idea of the height of your pet. Get a ruler and measure it. Were you right?